AF454354

SELF HELP

NEUROBICS

Women Empowerment COGNICARE

Dr Jaya Deshmukh & Dr Vandana Sharma

Chennai • Bangalore

CLEVER FOX PUBLISHING
Chennai, India

Published by CLEVER FOX PUBLISHING 2023

ISBN: 978-93-56483-97-2

INDEX

INTRODUCTION

The super power book SELF HELP NEUROBICS is here to empowering mind and energies. Especially for the young working women professionals, the cognitive skills are just like a blessing. The multitasking skills and overwork load pressures are common now a day. Here we are representing the cognitive behaviour therapy and neurolinguistic programming to advancing your personal growth. Your thought patterns are responsible for your actions and relations and success in life. You should take responsibility of your own failures and be strong enough to bounce back again. How is it possible to control emotions? Can you change our belief patterns easily? Why you are dependent on others for emotional support? Can you make a strong ecosystem for your personal success points? Yes everything is possible with self help neurobics. Yes now from today onwards, you don't have to depend on others at least for the emotional support. This book is equipped with proven principles of cognitive behaviour therapy, neurolinguistic reprogramming and energy healing concepts. The inspiration and encouragement everything is here to unlock true potential. Don't worry about the challenges and problems of life. You are enough to win every situation. Just learn the new better version of thought pattern and try to internalize the success principles. Why you are wasting time in entertainment and non intellectual works? Believe me the skills and wisdom have eternal bliss, go, get up, level up and speed up. I am sure this book will make you highly engaged in high proficiency words and works. Just do perfect creative visualization on each and every line of his book. The miracle vibrations will rearrange your inner matter, aura and universal connections. Trust the vibes and continue the magic manifestation effects of power feelings of this book.

Cognitive behaviour therapy and neurolinguistic reprogramming, both the techniques are excellent to make you realize the progressive mindset and advanced skill set. The drastic change and miracle manifestations are waiting for you. If you are ready to build rewarding life follow the commands of modules. No matter how many challenges you are facing, after the completion of this book reading, you will feel energetic and enough mature to deal big things in life forever. This book will empower you with time tested principles and that is the clear instruction to all of you, work on implementations on daily basis. Just 90 days creative visualisation and proper implementation will change you forever, far better than previous version of yourself.

What is the first and serious reason of procrastination and laziness? That is depression. There are so many individuals are there in our friends and family, who are found of depressive and aggressive attitude. They don't have spine to admit there mistake and cheatings. They are not enough mature to face the challenges with dignity and pride because of lack of mind powers and wisdom. The most obvious and typical sign of depression is a sad mood. Behavioural signs for clinical depression are fear, guilt and grief expressions. Constantly tired feelings and fibromyalgia are the 2 major problems of depression. The results of long term depressive state are hormonal imbalance, hypothyroidism, diabetes, PCOD, pre menstrual symptoms, post menopausal symptoms. Teen age girls to young adult girls to post menopausal age group women, all are very hard working and they have to do multitasking as family household works, education and job priority works, relationship issues and list is going on. If over work stress is there then we can't give our best to society and even the self care and self esteem also goes down. That's why we need a very supportive ecosystem to care the emotional needs of mind and nutritional balance of body.

Let's talk over solutions; what cognitive behavioural therapy suggests to solve abnormal behavioural signs (fear, stress, depression, anxiety and painful laziness).

This is a workbook and you can use it for self help and for others.

SPECIAL 10 MANNERS OF CBT NLP SESSIONS

Don't forget to use 10 manners of CBT NLP sessions. Amazing neuroplasticity will lead you on success path.

1. Slow command sessions; Don't try to read fast. You have to do creative visualisation on each and every statement. Perfect imaginations with celebration vibes are expected.

2. Creative visualisation cards; Take screenshots, pictures, images or at least clearly written goal cards will help you to revisit success points every day.

3. Brain boosters commands; Have list of 20 affirmations, use mirror technique to use them as commands to you. Give eye to eye contact and bold voice along with command.

4. Victory mindset vision board; Think about the problems and solutions and write them on vision board. If solutions are ready, it will promote you on speedy progress.

5. Excellent micro action steps; it would be very beneficial if you have clarity of all action steps, write down 1 to 100 each and every step with time limit.

6. Mindful strengthening of Commitments; Try to work with good accountability partners, they will keep you on track and you will stick to your daily commitments regarding goal completion. lllllll

7. High priority thoughts and actions; Every minute specific words and works are key to ultimate consistency and that type of consistency is the direct way to top goals.

8. Pride and peak performance strategies; if your strategies are clear, you will focus on them with conviction. You have to pay attention on several pride moments of extraordinary hard work during preparations.

9. Ultra clear conviction and reward system; If you are firm on every hour better quality efforts, that type of conviction will stimulate your brain reward system. It is a pure magic moment and time expansion will make space for you, so can do more in less time.

10. Unconscious competence & affirmations; don't ever settle for less than you deserve. Embrace your right to be rich and guarantee your financial well being by registering all the affirmations in all the levels of mind. Your continuous conscious efforts will give iceberg effect to subconscious mind powers. Subconscious mind power is the key of competence and after the 90 days, you will feel unconscious competence to reproduce affirmations exactly according to your mission.

20 STEPS FOR DAILY ROUTINE PRIORITIES

1. We generally recommend that you should take nutritional diet according to optimum required daily dose of minerals. Multivitamins and EPA DHA are also vital. No matter how, doesn't forget to take essential amino acids and co enzyme Q10 as vital supplements in daily diet.

2. Specially for prevention of alzheiemer's and sub acute combined degenerations take proper doses of vitamin B12 and folic acid along with lycopene.

3. Early morning cardio, brain gym and aerobics. Endorphins, adrenalines rush and cortisol balance will happen if you are ready to follow regular physical fitness regime.

4. Impart good values and establish value system; never go for compromises just for temporary pleasures. Always set a clear intention to express loyalty and sincerity. It's your responsibility to impart good values and virtues in your surroundings, never lose any opportunity to express and rebuild value system.

5. No procrastination no fear, get rid of every negative emotion; learn steps of amygdala hijack control, you will become fearless and bold to lead ahead an extraordinary hard working life.

6. Abstinence from toxic relations; detachment from all minor and major non target oriented things; high quality attachment with target oriented things. Ignore every toxic person, keep yourself away from them, always try to avoid any type of thoughts and talks about them.

7. Follow speed learning technique and learn new skills; make yourself extremely busy in new skills learning or advancement of existing mindset skill set. If you are focused and very attentive then no one can stop you from speed learning and implementing extra polished skills.

8. Internalize the commands and gratifications expression; kindly reinforce the fact that success is possible only through efforts and has no other shortcuts. You must take control over commands, have a sound revision of them, just internalised all the commands. Don't be lazy

and put extra efforts to express the pleasure especially when gained from the satisfaction after showing best efforts in massive quantity.

9. Wise and disciplined trained brain; You are trained, expert and genius that's fine. Now show your intellectual capacity to the world, perform well and communicate extra well. Your discipline will unlock true potential.

10. Passion will make you soul enrichment oriented; The soul is real life force, have complete belief on your actions and with expression of passion try to enhance the effects and impact of actions. That is the best way of soul nourishment with every action. Cherish it every day, don't miss the chance.

11. Extremely precious relations and celebrations; Always try to show the gratitude and respect for the special relations. It's your soul duty to give strong reasons to them for happiness and celebrations.

12. Self esteem and tremendous will power; the problems and failures are part of life. Try to bounce back as soon as possible, never stuck on any negative situation. If you are ready to fight with courage and conviction then only your self esteem will rise to set extra ordinary will power in your life.

13. Negative response replaced by witness consciousness; never give immediate reaction for any negative situation. Your response will decide your emotional maturity and try to prevent negative response with clear self control. See yourself as witness and have strong healing vibes to find solutions.

14. Highly selective orientations- every hour winner mindset; victory mindset is the key to make every hour highly productive. You can trust on your basic instinct regarding highly selective about time, place, person and standards.

15. Sympathetic control and joyful relaxation; Fear, flight, fright, fight and aggression, anxiety everything is just a sign of sympathetic over charging that's why you need a parasympathetic stimulation and harmonious life style. The sympathomimetic and parasympathomimetic balance is essential. Deep sleep and relaxation is must. Insomnia and over work load are the main causes of psychosomatic disorders.

16. Harmony of relations and giving mode on; don't be selfish, think about the needs of others and try to give your best possible support and focus on proper care and concerns. If everyone is very supportive to each other then no one will feel depression. The harmony of relation is must to secure better energy alignment and greater manifestations.

17. No blame no demands, just send best wishes; the blame game is the root cause of every bad relation. Over demanding nature is the most common cause of disturbed harmony. Forgiveness and gratitude are 2 best solutions to calm down your mind. Now from today onwards just believe in no revenge rule. You have to obey the rule and send best wishes to everyone.

18. Unconditional help and no credit expectations; Remember you have to serve others and no matter what, have to go for help beyond expectations. Don't even try to demand credit or attention. The real pride and joyful gestures are gifts of unconditional love and support. Your extra ordinary help will help someone to make big decisions of life. Cherish all the moments of unconditional help.

19. Revisit, reimagine, recreat better affection moments; Loyalty the best policy. Never waste time in emotional drama and fears and fights. Just focus on your excellent hard work, dedications, special care and concerns about each and every person of family. You have to redesign your plan, go for it and make your destiny better than previous.

20. Never say die and just enjoy excellent creativity in present moment with current massive sure success efforts. Have a track record of efforts and every day get better and better than earlier. Follow the high quality KAP and enjoy advance skills. KAP (knowledge, attitude and practises).

10 MODULES are here in this book. Every module contains 20 pointers to hit the target buttons of advanced cognitive behaviour skills.

The cognitive skills pointers are ready to enhance the mind power. All super hit commands of workshop are here; just make use of them and enjoy instant transformation. If you need help to understand the pointers; we are always ready to help you, feel free to contact us.

Workshops webinars and master classes everything is here to support you. If you have problem regarding translation. The workshops are available in Hindi and English, both languages. So join in and get started on the transformation for best version of yourself.

INSIGHT & INTENTION RECTIFICATION

Insight & intention rectification; maintain the stability; if your intentions are great, they will purify your insights. Always be ready to rectify them, even if there are little low standard you find. You have to maintain a calmness and stability so no one can disturb you or distract you from the best insights points. Try to understand the intentions of others, never say they are wrong in aggressive mode. Have a gentle response that you know the wrong intentions of them, that's why all the feelings and dealings are stopped. Just ignore them and stay away from them. Protect yourself from the blame gamers.

1. Irresistible women; sense of accomplishment; truly inspired women have irresistible momentum to sense and complete all the accomplishments on time. Being irresistible is about being comfortable with who you are. You are enough. Yes everything is beautiful in you. Inside to outside you can win anything you want.

2. Unstoppable leadership; extra supportive nurturing environment; from today onwards you are going more connected to your future to establish success as soon as possible

3. Content programming; extremely important and satisfactory; your new personality is going to connect with supporters and well wishers. Highly expected success moments are close to you. Read the cognitive commands with extremely satisfying feelings. Celebrate your future success in present moment, at present moment.

4. Micro moment alert automation; exert yourself little beyond comfort zone; read the emotions and learn from the moral judgement success stories. The stories, case studies and develop intuitive ability. Learn about the right pattern of judgement and rich vibes of trust

bonds. The energy exchange with excellent group discussion will improve social interaction ability. That type of talk therapy will increase your endorphin and dopamine level in mind.

5. Peak performance enlightening; skill set mindset harmony; speech therapy for teen agers. They need intellectual vocabulary on daily basis to satisfy adrenaline rush, to remove cravings of addiction and unwanted entertainment.

6. Before time & chief influencer; user's guide reference daily; Thicker and denser neuronal connection will improve brain powers. Cognitive workouts are excellent to force you towards the best purpose of your life.

7. Seriously better than previous accountability; Keep your eyes on better version of yourself. That is nothing but a sign indicating that you want to live a life of meaning and substance. The matter of accountability in terms of better contributions quality check is essential.

8. Organised blissful ecosystem; handle conflicts without hurt; self control during revengeful situations is must. Keep yourself in no revenge zone; focus on your higher value system. Show excellent self discipline and talk as matured enough solution mastery thought expert.

9. Target orientation and ceremony; bridge the gap between desires and achievements. Always celebrate the little targets completions. The orientation is to help others with value added services are enough to bridge the gap between desires and achievements of self and others. Work for the dreams of others, never say you are alone and think about the needs of others also.

10. Inculcation of virtues and values; spiritual wellbeing. You are a divine being in human form. Apply work ethics to maintain values. Regulation of nervous system depends on organised thought pattern is essential to understand. We have to follow the values and maintain a harmony between workplace excellence and personal growth targets.

11. Altruism promotional discipline; hard earned wisdom; utilize every point of content and experience massive shift every day.

12. Cherish responsibility and glow; fame with soul enrichment. The advance skills are

13. Energy appreciation and exchange; efforts with refining wellness shift

14. Humble and Advanced skilful gestures; ready to work in emergency; completely satisfied with universal support to face challenges without any depression and aggression.

15. Access denied for low vibes relations; avoid lazy bees and their poor vibes culture; believe in your ability to achieve anything.

16. Extra ordinary energy level hours; avoid procrastinations ; know crystal clear action steps; go fast to next level as soon as possible.

17. Horizontal and vertical integration of success mantras; don't change the chain of priority thought pattern; feel 100% confident to chase after your dreams.

18. Focus on present and incredible 2 minutes rule; Give excellent focus and best concerns on what is in front of you; be closer than ever to realizing your true potential.

19. Get up; Level up; speed up; on super selective matter see every area of your life increase in value better than surroundings; shift your ecosystem and reach at better higher vibes place.

20. Show massive optimism to bounce back and move ahead with better than previous speed. Never feel inadequate or unworthy again. Experience complete faith again.

LEAD AND WIN WITH JOY AND GLORY

Next hill top as soon as possible; Show your work efficiency and glow. With a mission statement, we can flow with the betterment ideas. Don't stuck anywhere in between, the consistency is expected from you. Don't allow anyone to hold you or distract you. You don't need to figure out everything and everybody in order to accommodate and adjust according to their standard. If you want to win, just maintain security based on high self esteem acquired after the tremendous efforts. Then only you will become unstoppable and no one will challenge your position on vibes ground.

1. Declutter detox and detachments; don't engage in toxic culture, no need to discuss about your weak points or action plans to everyone. Keep some secrets and show your final results. Do extra ordinary preparations. Detach yourself from every low vibe. Don't waste time in toxic relationships. Go out of the dirty zone and never join again the blame gamers low class standards. Understand the power of walking away from less supportive energies. Just get declutter everything that doesn't serve your purpose.

2. Enhance potential and selective vibes only; team efforts with accountability. Where is your vision board, road map and every hour credit score board? You cannot finish all tasks on time if you don't have accountability and authenticity value system. Keep yourself updated with selective approach to unlock all hidden potential. Keep in touch with team members and mentors, they will hold your hand and you will run very fast on success path.

3. Passion pro enthusiasm corner; Finish all the micro tasks before time. Be a passion pro and rock every day. The enthusiasm to hold wisdom moments will lead you on most speedy path of success. Yes it will become spark and catalyst to enhance all powers.

4. Miracle and manifestations flames; revision and reimaging better than previous; do revisions and recall sessions again and again, to cherish clarity and conviction. Then only the process and product will glow by your sincere practice.

5. Essential Regime & Prediction; work schedule fix and flexible on specific matters;

6. Express better value system; no revenge and no negative reply only genuine respect

7. Strongest desires upholding; Mentor and expert 60 x 60 in your mind.

8. Gracefully 'Lead and learn'; new level of learning and teaching with hand holding leadership manner

9. Biggest creativity implementation high tricks; give them equal opportunity to make pride performance

10. Joyful glory of every command; follow the work ethics and respect the guidelines

11. Extra disciplined massive micro actions; benefits and rewards oriented push and pull

12. Beyond limitation redesign aspect; flow of unpredictable but supportive elements

13. Consistent efforts speedy progress; high productivity energy attraction

14. Neurobics Fast commands Power; achieve amazing and feel connected with your true genius self

15. Cognitive Excellence Reflection; respect and love yourself again

16. Higher Temperaments speed reading; Don't stuck in conflicts

17. Super conscious Dominant talks; Transcendent intuitions

18. High Alert active awareness; healing codes reopen them right now

19. Support yourself make worth fortune; Daily focused morning

20. Eating and thinking with rhythm; no vacation craving; higher vitality with no fatigue zone

SIGNIFICANT EFFORTS ENHANCEMENT; ENERGY EXPANSION

Significant efforts enhancement; No depression no grief excuses, only target oriented steps with high speed sigma rule. Understand the papez circuit, brain reward system and insular cortex sensations, everything is clearly mentioned in book Sanskar. That is the only way to understand the high speed sigma rule. We are lucky that we can up regulate the gene expressions with emotional well being activities. The great researches are already here to establish the reversal of diseases and reduction of complications with the energy and emotion based cognicare principles. You are smart enough to understand the importance of reprogramming and rewiring of thoughts.

Change your belief patterns, change behaviour and make a legacy.

1. Tremendous Exaggeration link words; inner tranquil sanctuary. The inner tranquillity means a safest sanctuary where super mind powers are there to support you. Learn the anchor method and with the excellent use of link words, enhance the emotional upliftment. Avoid the negative events stupid recall pattern and just focus on tremendous positivity and massive progress in your cognitive skills.
2. Maximize deep affection busy bees; rejuvenation and anti-aging joy vibes. Your connection with your well wishers is of so much importance. Stay connected and do frequent meet ups to rejuvenate the inner beautiful energies. Believe in supernatural ability of genes to heal fast.
3. Go out of the way; out of the box; stay consistent 1000 pages self help guide. Don't give attention to non target oriented things. Literally consistently knock on the genetic door and break out the normal thinking pattern.

4. Show "make it happen" passion; Awaken your limitless creation power. You are the designer of your own destiny. You are a genetic engineer, in the present moment, with the specific high vibe thought, you can heal anything.

5. Show and glow; make accurate decisions; access to supportive ecosystem and expression of full creation powers; You are a consumer, be selective about each and everything, consume thoughts and things only of high quality. Never compromise on quality and standards. Great creative powers are there in your mind, get up move on and stay ahead always with your best possible creations.

6. Instant massive shifts Schedule; more comprehensive approach. According to your best targets, make proper schedule to approach next level success. Your approach will make you better than others, remember that.

7. Greatest degree of creative visualisation; significant dedication to encourage your commitment

8. Orders and organizations super authentic; Gratitude towards the self help commands revisit sessions

9. Greatest Wisdom Expression ease; Tough gets going & going gets tough.

10. Transform your insecurities into bliss

11. Elevated emotions to unlock potential and feel polarised to create long term memory

12. Highly charged moments ; Highly influential auto talks; 5000 commands for 10 days

13. Repetitive metaphors ; incredible impact on others;

14. Grow resiliency; keep your cool; earn best respect and avoid conflicts arguments insulting points.

15. Don't lose temper otherwise you will lose best long term interest

16. Manage challenging situations gracefully and affectionately

17. If they don't have respect for your persona then never show your anger, ignore them with full loyalty and with very sincere and dedicated approach mind your own business.

18. Avoid being the victim because of negligence and non supportive attitude of others. You are no longer passive and lazy; show your excellent solution oriented approach. Great growing and glowing elements will increase in your success journey by taking full control and ownership.

19. Fix each and every component of problem and appreciate each and every angle of automated direct healing system.

20. V5 V6 visual cortex occipital lobe stimulation; more visionary more fulfilling ,higher priority engaged mindset

MICROMANAGE THE MICROACTION STEPS; FINE FANTANCY MODE

Keep your attention on the process. Break down the bigger goal into manageable tasks and put each effort with extra skill set. Discover how you too can ignite the natural confidence, you were born with to unlock limitless possibilities and become unstoppable in just 90 days. Let go of past failures. Become your own advocate and get ready to step into the best version of yourself. Try better mindset, Even if you have tried everything else before and failed, no matter, try again. Win the final game once again.

Just declare that I want unstoppable confidence; as I have to help others.

1. Understand spiritual perspective and attain the ultimate purpose of targets. Think about time place and person and go ahead with better orientation.
2. More distractions are signs of weak mindset. Developing focus for long hours is the key to maintain intense focus; write down quality quantity and speed of target oriented actions.
3. Try to highlight each and every faulty thought pattern. Never do insult and don't create blame game. With due respect try to enhance comfortable environment to improve all faults and mistakes. Do better practice every time and reduce the probability of mistakes.
4. Emotional entrainment and influence patterns;
5. Self discipline and flow of neuroplasticity excellence
6. Amygdala and its connections to association area of the visual cortex are responsible for recall of fear factors again and again; break the chain; replace them with target oriented action

7. Emotional neglect and emotional support synchrony. Impulse control Self growth.
8. Altruism will lead you on the path of advanced skill set and mindset; its importance is need of the day and to maintain loyalty towards goals oriented words
9. 100 value words every weekend celebration; cognicare weekend celebration
10. Fast and effortless attraction of prosperity
11. Immediate workflow and high speed zone
12. Crystal clear target oriented approach; genuinely feeling honoured with fast command sessions
13. Raise your standard to uplift instant next level approach
14. Talks and walks to explore more with clarity and conviction.
15. Keep IIO work with great respect; Ignore Irrelevant Objects.
16. Low priority words and works; strict awareness and time saving mindset
17. Stimulation of prefrontal cortex and brain reward system manipulations
18. Overcome obstacles with overlook blame gamers tasks; no distraction zone
19. Glow with present time purposeful activity and grow with extra passion ; love the process of success
20. Fly above clouds; don't argue with fools

FREE FLOW MODE AND HIGH FLY ZONE

Fly High and don't break the flow; don't stuck anywhere; just proceed ahead with complete ownership of your sure success blueprint. On the path of success, there will be many obstacles and no matter what you have to run with your best speed. Don't forget the hands of well wishers, the blessings of your new soul connections are always there to uplift you. Maintain the peak performance every day and never say die before the completion of tasks. Go dear grow fast and glow more with great insights and divine blessings. Spread your wings fly high and enjoy the free flow bliss effect.

1. The universe brought you here today for a reason. The beautiful soulful relation with universal power is the top secret thing to manipulate the game plan in your favour. The other one near you still wondering the divine bliss is your easy tasks. Enjoy the divine bliss and maintain the perception bliss effect in every win win situation.

2. You desperately need a place to escape from all toxic bites, to recharge, to rejuvenate, to replenish better future version of yourself. The toxic relations are like viruses, killing you and your dream, immediately set big goals and go away from all stupid fellows, no matter if they are part of family. Leave them right now, with complete detachment and strong mind move ahead.

3. Abundance affluence and new wealth of limitless fortune; The new world of fortune, in terms of perfect relations, good financial status and blissful home and environment of workplace, everything is for you. Believe in it and you are going to achieve everything.

4. The purposeful vibrant mind and radiant cells of body; harmony in action. The Super power of words are magical, you have ability to do creative visualisation on every life changing

idea. Those types of vibrations are vital to thrive again. The bounce back is not enough, You have to show harmony in every talk and walk as you are already blessed with divine love and support.

5. The vibrational phenomenon of sigma thoughts; deep believer in destiny manipulations. The most beautiful thing in the world is the sigma thoughts. It means you are satisfied with your values and virtues and no matter what going to celebrate life of abundance with all of loved ones. Earn massively, donate gracefully and give the best possible contribution for the betterment of society.

6. Forgive, forget and erase now the unfortunate events of recent and past; give incredible intention set points for future promotions. Your future version is very beautiful and beyond appreciation greatness is glowing on it. Give the power of intentions to present works and according to better version finish all the tasks within time limit.

7. If you found yourself falling into same lazy patterns of cycle; say strict no to worst days of life. Sometimes the depression and aggression is on prime factor position and person cannot move ahead because of poor judgement ability. Never allow them to destroy your moods and days. The worst days are no more now; you are capable enough to fight for your best rights.

8. The universe preparing you to feel all boundaries of your existence evaporate as you are welcomed in an ocean of possibility and promise

9. Feel the force of creative visualisations; Stick to best possible destiny manipulation minutes. Lazy crazy moments are the signs of foolish fellows, be aware and alert, don't waste emotions for unfaithful things. Think better and maintain the standard quality hard work to support your destiny. The manipulations are in demand and the facilitators are welcomed. Go ahead and do wonderful creations.

10. The next better achievement of life presented itself to you; grace the occasion; embrace the opportunity. I deserve the best and I have right to keep relation with better vibes person, I have full right to ignore stupid fellows.

11. Neuronal rhythms and universal vibes common plan; influencing and proving to be more powerful than we ever realized. Your high quality thoughts are creating miracle, attracting universal support from excellent resource makers, be alert and try to grab the best opportunities, maintain the neuronal rhythm of 7777 thoughts miracle booster effect.

12. Now the neuroplasticity miracles, randomly felt by you are extremely similar to those of lifelong monks that claim to have reached enlightenment. But the problem is your doubtful

attitude and validation seeking talks. You are ready to waste time in low priority actions, instead investing energy and attention on long hours of deep meditation. Immediately stop all previous low vibes activities. Filter everything and through the garbage as soon as possible.

13. Life started to become beautiful for you from that moment; hyper consciousness; profound unaltered state of awakening. The perfect stability and never ending enthusiasm to explore matters of personal progress. Yes the beauty of unaltered untouched supreme nature is the key to ultimate success.

14. You have to attribute towards a symphony of vibrating strings; iceberg effect will attract gratitude and respect you deserve. Don't worry if your hidden qualities are taking time to explore out or no one is there to appreciate your virtues, have patience the talent and extra ordinary efforts will make you shine on every ground. Just maintain the high vibes of self esteem and continue all great works better then past performances.

15. You have to understand that the grace of prosperity can only be accessed in very specific conditions; get your mind into a state known as theta.

16. When your mind is in this heightened state your subconscious mind is wide open now to absorb manifestations instantly.

17. Your mind and all the relevant matters and elements of sure success in the universe is made up of vibrations that are genuinely trying to synchronize; adjust the synchrodestiny with immediate effects; stop synchronising with all of the negative events in life and start synchronising with positive future expectations and events.

18. Start harnessing the power of transformations; vibrations can do miracle right now ; have strong faith on ability to transform by your own thoughts and action, just maintain a higher standard of intellectual talks and greater feelings.

19. Trigger the theta state and understand the sound healing of inner voice; genius genome expression enhancement; better possibilities and make it possible attitude. Focus on inner voice and micro-manage the time. That is the perfect trigger for theta state. When you are ready to create best moments then only gene expressions will change itself for better.

20. Embrace your true destiny; expand your reality with every command of genius genome module. Follow the mastery modules of GMC CN; Genius mind consultancy by Cognicare Neurobics. The critical thinking and proper learning environment is essential to work on higher priority actions.

MAGNETIC COGNITIVE COMMANDS: HIGHLY ORGANISED MANNER

Be Magnetic with self love; No matter what, sad or bad is the situation just give respect to your identity. Each and every action is very beautiful, if you consider yourself as especial persona. After all you have to face everything by your own and you cannot afford unnecessary emotional drama. Don't set compromising mode just for responsibilities. Your success is your responsibility. Never demand external support from unorganised fellows, no matter if they are the part of family, just take care of them and go to your business. Set special thought pattern and work on higher goals, as the goals are on prime priority. High priority actions are always in demand and you have to set example of that expectation.

1. Don't go for validations; keep your decisions and choices in your control. That is your birth right to enjoy freedom. If you want to change something, No one can stop you. Go ahead and be your change. You are not a puppet of anyone. Only you can change your life, no one can do it for you.

2. Keep distance from false ego and false belief pattern; otherwise you will fall apart in blame game pit. Stop suffering because of ego trip. The person, who wants to help you, will leave you, if you are not ready to change old- sad- false belief patterns.

3. Recognizing all the powerful skill and developing ability to express them well; you are born with genius mindset, have strong belief and now make yourself highly expressive. Why hesitations and why not bold expressions; as you are the owner of virtues and high value system. Enough is enough dear; go get up and run fast on your success roadmap.

4. Immense practice is possible only with high priority actions; you need supportive mentor to modify current state. The present situation is good, but you have to make it more powerful and worthy for massive success. Talk to your mentor, follow all the instructions very sincerely and show your excellent practice sessions to other well wishers. They will learn from your immense hard work and you will feel beautiful self worth again.

5. Energy portals work better in high vibes ecosystem; learn to maintain high command zone of affirmations. Every day give 20 minutes focused time and attention to read affirmations. Make them crystal clear and target oriented. Believe me just 20 minutes magic will change your entire life, if you follow this pattern for next 21 days consistently.

6. Make a list of prior habits that destroy your time energy and confidence; you need to immediately stop engaging in habits that are actually destroying self progress. Sometimes the poor relationship bonds and low priority actions are wasting your energy and you are not aware of this point. So set a clear boundary, don't allow anyone to destroy your confidence.

7. You have to project an effortless sense of self assurance and pretend that you can stand out in crowd wherever you go. The problem of self doubt is always there to trouble you, but here is the perfect solution exists in rule of pretend game. The initial few days you have to pretend that you have complete faith on your capabilities and after some days that will become your reality. The self assurance is a very powerful tool and be ready to shine by your own light.

8. Always have enough cognitive commands to approach and solve challenges in different ways; ultimately instant shift the odds in your favour and attract result according to your wish. Your old solutions are not working, that's why you have lack of confidence. Learn about the cognitive commands and think about the different better ways to approach. The better cognitive skills will help to create excellent solutions.

9. Truly confident state with high quality standard of talks and walks are in demand. The world of entertainment and distractions are not good always. The focus is not on self growth. The attention is not on high priority actions. Why roaming here and there without any solid purpose. Don't waste your precious time; don't give attention to meaningless distractions and purposeless entertainments. Your talks and walks should be based on high value system and then only you will feel state of truly confident mind.

10. Don't seek attention; don't show signs of desperate demands. Feel enough independence and capable outlooks to fulfil desires and need, without support from others. When you ask for attention, which will destroy your self esteem, you cannot glow in front of them. You have so many goals to accomplish. Your mentors and teams are waiting for you, now forget

about the little desires and have strong desire to succeed every hour with extra efforts. Give your best contribution and help others to fulfil accomplishments

11. Take active interest in learning new advance skills; stay calm and connected with divine bliss. It's hard to believe in your ability to accomplish something you have never attempted before, especially when your old track record is not for advanced setups. Now from today onwards keep remember thought patterns can be changed, just keep your vision clear; do every hour little better than before and record betterment with unstoppable conviction. You are capable of visualizing yourself achieving advancement in any specific skill.

12. Diffuse the hot situations; learn to give ignorant looks to low vibes critics; just keep your eye on clear vision of the bigger picture. When you decide to leave blame gamers far behind, when you are determined to ignore critics, when you are busy with the team of self help magicians, it would become very easy to avoid any hot situation not meant to you. Your bigger goals are in front you, work for them and leave everything untouched.

13. Problem solving better than previous approaches are vital to overcome unseen fears; as a result keep yourself well prepared and well equipped to navigate your way around hurdles and difficulties. The unseen fears are not known to you, but the cognitive skills are enough to face any fear or challenge. Make sure you are doing repeated revisions. To keep you updated and expert to use all cognicare tools; many modules are already present; just go through them and move with high speed.

14. Take the risk and go ahead with comfortable extraordinary peak performance mode; show every time and grow with every action.

15. You are not new in the field of competition; you have excellent experiences of future success points; your creative visualisation is on the top creativity mode; do our best work and leave the stage with power words.

16. Understand the great force of sound of inner healing vibes and voices. Go beyond the world; focus on source of incredible wisdom; feel the existence of universal supportive flow.

17. Reverberating process is going on in high vibes zone. Reverberate means the sound waves of your fast commands session travelling back and forth, as in an echo to transform you inside and out. The best echoing of progressive realisations will become the mind power; just keep yourself engaged in supercharged pattern. Be careful don't allow anyone to disturb you. Stay connected to source of wisdom and source of personal growth master. Now from today onwards, No outsider is allow to disturb you.

18. Mastery school codes are in your genes and mind; deep memories are already there; have a sense of perception and expression; then only your talent will work for you to find and attract best possible results for you. Harmonic structure of confidence building words will lead you on best possible heights of achievements.

19. Phenomenonal human dynamo persona is the result of your past perfect visualisation, now don't forget to recall and repeat all powerful points of wisdom, already created and established in your high vibes zone.

20. Keep high alert mode for every single action; you are very honest with yourself. It will also help you to regain control over your life. Remember that your actions and every little decision; always up to you. Have a firm belief and make sure the flow is smooth and speedy on success path, and without the contamination from low vibes.

BOUNCE BACK AND GROW FAST; BE UNSTOPPABLE

The bounce back capacity is essential to grow fast; you cannot waste time in depression and frustration. You have a fundamental right to disconnect from people that send you negative or ordinary vibes. Stop the stuck mentality, move fast and use success self talks as reminders for instant mind glow. There is always a faster way to freedom and a way to accelerate your healing and a pathway to unlock hidden potential. Don't forget to unblock neural connections. Relax, quiet your mind and begin amplifying your abundance with every statement of this module. Have complete belief that you are in zone of beautiful manifestations, getting world renowned success materials, global networked community of like-minded individuals, waiting to see what you are about to accomplish. Enjoy your success journey with ease joy and glory.

1. Insecurities are the main cause of frustration; now feel secured enough as you are well prepared and well supported by your divine instincts.
2. Failures and wrong decisions are just events of past; don't give attention and time to your past; bounce back; forget about past and go ahead with clear success points of future version of yourself.
3. Everything in your life is going to change; when you are ready to step into better ecosystem; you have to leave your older version completely; the old trauma and painful events are now not present here; welcome the new you is waiting to glow and grow.
4. Sometimes the faults, guilt and grief everything is there in mind to disturb peace of mind. The self acceptance is also not supporting; this painful situation is very dreadful and self pity is further makes you down; please remember, no matter what you have to face the negative

situations without any depression and frustration; if this thing is clear then no one will stop you to win and rock.

5.   The conversation you have to design and deep respect for every supporter you have, will transform you at any cost; remember with the grace of gratitude and respectful response you can win any battle.

6.   You have to accept yourself with all imperfections, don't feel inferiority complex as you are not weak and timid to break and cry again and again; feel the strength of your power words and feeling of self care.

7.   Everyone is fighting unseen battle and no one is getting full support but the self help neurobics are powerful to keep you on track without external motivation and external forces of sympathy.

8.   The fear of abandonment we all have, but it's our tolerance power to accept if someone doesn't like to continue. Take full responsibility of self love and joy and don't ask for anything to anyone.

9.   The world is full of excellent supporters and your space is the key factor to attract well wishers; if you are busy in negative thinking and blame game; that means you are making toxic vibes in your space and now no good person will join you. Keep distance from all blame gamers and manipulators just keep your space clean and clear for new soul connections.

10.   Multitasking and early finishers target points; Do not afraid of multitasking; keep harmony between all high yield tasks; after all you have to fulfil all responsibilities and have to move ahead with high speed to finish big targets of purposeful success.

11.   You have to become best listener in the world; but make sure that you have to listen carefully only target oriented actions and talks. Listen to your mentors; listen to your inner voice; listen to self help commands; and most important listen to your better version.

12.   Create more peaceful and progressive world around you. When the enhanced potential is there in every ones skill set and mindset; no one will fight for financial issues. Everyone is busy to perform best efforts to support each other; then no point will remain constant to create dispute and conflicts.

13.   Create a clear vision for yourself and be the change that is required to maintain the transformation.

14.   Show your compassion to needy and poor. Give time, energy, attention, affection and respect to each and every one who is around you, as you have to create high vibes and high emotional attachments in your ecosystem where everyone can nourish and flourish.

15. Never allow your memories to use you. Forget the ego issues and revengeful points. Set a better pride moment and every time create a better perception and pride.

16. You are not a victim of anyone's story. You are beyond the reach of blame gamers and haters. Feel free to shine, feel ease to come out of comfort zone; rise again and never return to low quality standards.

17. Grace over grudges is always matter the most. Try to give responses with grace. Grace the occasion and give response with all intellectual points.

18. Disagreements are ok but disrespect is very bad, those types of toxic vibes are very harmful and never allow toxicity around you. Silence is the loudest reply you can give. Never keep fear and revenge in mind; just avoid toxic talks and keep high grade solitude in your meaningful life.

19. Be bold enough to stand in front of haters; honour your scars and don't hide them; they have no right to judge you and don't allow anyone to put opinion about you. Have enough pride that you are going to create massive success in front of them.

20. Hardship and consistent efforts are the stage show points; always keep your eye on targets, mind your best business and become busy bee for better skill presentation. Your super selective works will make progress for you.

PROTECTION IS BETTER THAN CURE; SELECTIVE SUPPORTIVE ECOSYSTEM

Failure to protect yourself and not able to defend your subordinate, is the direct sign of weakness; work on it and stand out for the honour of your tribe. Maintain joint efforts and highly supportive environment for each other. Try to enhance energy level, work on skills development. The advance skill presentations and collective healing will cherish every name and fame.

1. You will always be judged for what you say and how you respond; so focus on high standard responses ; make your impact so powerful to show the highest value system you possess enough.

2. Don't chase anyone; the vibrational standard you established is very high to align with low vibes tribes. If they want to go away, let them do this separation peacefully as you need a special space for special supportive new soul connections.

3. 100 pages are ready to transform your life, read every page 10 times, do creative visualization deeply, feel excellent transformation and be super selective to talks and walks.

4. No matter how much alone you are never reconnect with toxic person; don't make any deal with blame gamers.

5. Maintain quiet outlooks and complete silence but never give negative reply as everyone has so much pain inside, be kind and leave them if they are not your well wishers, but never hurt in return; take better revenge, just ignore them without hesitation and enjoy better success with better tribe.

6. Work on yourself; sometimes strangers will support and anytime the false ego relations will behave like blame gamers; never underestimate the self discipline and self worth. Don't stop again to give reply to blame gamers and do high speed work.

7. Don't ruin the garden by thinking about the thorns. Just because it's taking time doesn't mean it's not happening. You have to understand the tough competition as long hours of daily efforts for many years, really a difficult job. But never lose hope, one day the result will come to bless you massively.

8. You will become what you constantly think about, watch yourself with every command and have conviction with every effort. Every day 50 minutes of highly dedicated moments for this vital work, are enough to proceed ahead with great leap.

9. Your growth will skyrocket if your all micro actions are full of sigma (better than previous efforts) rules; Don't waste your entire life to wait for right time. Just put all the excellent efforts and create high vibes to attract best possible achievements instantly.

10. Bees don't waste their time explaining to flies that honey is better than shit. If the blame gamers are busy in shit like works, don't waste times to teach them anything, just create honey like sweet and meaningful product and leave them on their own box.

11. Don't tell anyone, what you are doing until it's done. Outside energy can throw off goals. Not every person is happy with your success, keep silent zone around you and show them massive results after the task completion.

12. Hurt, hate, reactions, panic and blame all 5 points are enough to break you from inside to outside. That's why you have to protect yourself from haters. Keep a distance from the trigger persons or past pointers; otherwise you will get trapped again in low vibes cycle.

13. Stand guard at the door of your mind. listen well and speak for the skills and wisdom, leave the silly matters and cheap fights because your time is precious and stop scaring yourself with negative predictions ; give assurance and concerns to every one

14. Your thoughts and feelings are going to universe and come back to you multiplied. Self control and self regulation is always essential to perform our target oriented tasks even in boring or problematic situation.

15. Statistics and medical reports are not based on mind powers and healing miracles; don't feel sad about the past failures of psychosomatic disorders. You have to work on healing and subconscious miracles and you can transform your life up to the highest point of success.

16. The big screen is in front of you, write down the answers and make it happen every miracle right now. The achievements you want to show to your community are already get watched in big screen of mind;

17. The challenges are there to judge you; it's your response bitter, bad and ugly or sweet, polite and graceful with gratitude. Feeling sad and upset and don't want to give affection and appreciation; no matter how rude you can behave, but listen carefully you have to create extraordinary achievements for everyone.

18. You are the creator of your own destiny. Make sure the best possible creations as soon as possible. Show the signs of urgency and finish all the creations within time limit.

19. If you didn't get celebrated enough; start celebrating every little effort; give enough gratitude to yourself for every day cares and concerns and responsibilities. Always behave like a genius who don't like to waste things and time in low vibes.

20. The little thing could make a big difference. Give your best possible attention and concern to higher priority action and step by step go ahead, don't take rest in between. Complete a big target in one shot.

SIGNATURE PHRASES; DECLARATION REWARD PHENOMENA

Now according to next module we have to learn about the 20 steps of next fast command session; Surprising Benefits of signature phrases. The most important question is 'are you ready'. Keep yourself in pure conscious awareness and go for huge transformation. Make yourself little uncomfortable and focus on extremely deep work. Don't try to control everything, just follow zero response zones. You have to act, only on high priority action. No need to do blame or complaint. Don't ask stupid questions. Don't behave to show false ego and false belief.

1. Subconscious mind powers are perfectly able to respond conscious words. Just talk with conviction and move to next step with full faith in current step. Step into the next level of your own power confidence

2. Be a solitude loving personality; not easily accessible energy point; not always available genius; exclusive high priority action producing persona. Subconscious flow is the result of repetitions of ultimate sure success concepts. The repetitions are the best stimulator; make sure the feelings and vibrations are also there to accept bliss.

3. Enhance your tolerance power and have focused attention on processing of iceberg phenomena.

4. The very first step of CBT is understand the PTSD affects and conditioning impacts; now proceed to a treatment protocol

5. Always remember the neuronal synopsis you are making during reading and creative visualization; is the first and last vital point of long lasting feel deal heal cycle.

6. Stimuli entry points are visual, audio and subliminal; now take concerns about stages. Visual stimuli are easy to understand but make your perceptions up to the mark to cherish subliminal signs. Sound healing with binaural beats is the key point system to stimulate auditory cortex. Now understand the stages of stimuli appreciation and implementation facilitation.

   6.1. Initiation stage and antivirus effect; The haters and toxic vibes creators are around you. Learn the protective measures and create auric shield. The initiation is a very tough phenomenon and when you have lack of support system, it's become most difficult tasks to face challenges. But don't worry; you have antivirus thought pattern if you are on practice of cognicare neurobics.

   6.2. Preparation stage and clarity genome;

   6.3. Peak of experience and catalyser effect;

   6.4. Repeat the anchor and avoid the trigger;

   As per the 4 stages of stimuli cognitive influence; you have to rewire you brain for future destiny points. Live the dream while minimizing your risks and maximizing your success.

7. Strategies that really work are in front of you; now everything depends on passion and facilitation. Open up your mind to receiving every manifestation to transform outcome as best possible result for you.

8. The unconscious competence and talks. Deepest desires are ready to explore the world. Do so much practice and repetitions and make it happen with your divine mind powers. Just maintain the spark to do more and more every day. Go extra miles every day. Set extraordinary action steps and allow yourself to feel honour with each action step.

9. Energy healing automation pro cess and authenticity. Think about your capacity and ability. Do you really deserve the best? What kind of plan you have? Are you ready to go through and grow through with every challenge? If you answers are up to the mark and really according to highest calling then congratulations, now you will achieve super success very soon.

10. Realize shift 10 x and reinvent your better part. What clutter is entering in your mind? You are not in ease and not doing things in order to priority? That's why there is diseases and disorders. Think better and act better and don't repeat old standards. Have a complete belief in your efforts. Make sure new standards and new better version of preparations are ready to rock.

11. Intellectual consulting industry; unconsciously competent NLP practitioner. Random thoughts and unorganised actions are the main reason of energy and emotion bliss blockers. Specific, high value, highly organised thoughts are key points.

12. To learn about proficiency and neuronal memory and energy vibes bank; trust your inner voice. Appreciate the solitude. The power of silence is great. You will discover massive manifestations just by trusting the inner voice. The thought patterns are changing every day as you are committed to proficiency visualization sigma rules. Congratulate yourself to making new neuronal manners to establish long lasting memories for peak performances in future.

13. Do not break the rhythm; horizontal and vertical integration always on every success points; Be a lifelong learner. Learn the techniques of advance skill development, every day in every manner just extra points to your knowledge and skill. Keep your vibes high to work with big projects oriented executives.

14. High focus zone is equal to no distraction zone; that's why increase the focus and attention and think with logical mind, now read the consequences. See you have to write the consequences of not doing high priority micro actions. Now keep yourself in no distraction zone. Always remember your priority is to maintain full focus on win win attitude.

15. Eradicate all weak points; don't give too much attention on emotional drama created by blame gamers; ask for deep yearning and firm resolve. No one is perfect in the world, no need to entertain imposter syndrome. Just take a deep breath and go ahead to resolve all the matters. No need to give reply to any lazy or crazy fellow. You have full right to avoid emotional fools.

16. To show your tremendous efforts have strong belief in immense potential; follow the evidence based approach. You are not aware of your extra ordinary potential, that's why you are afraid to take risk or to do beyond limit initiatives. First of all unlock the potential with alpha training and then enjoy the free flow of massive efforts from your side.

17. Spark of curiosity; astonishing effects of meaningful tasks. Just like a child you are curious about everything and like an adult you want to know about more meaningful things. You cannot afford a casual manner to approach anything. Keep your approach really excellent and amazing to enhance astonishing effects.

18. Sensorimotor psychotherapy modules are enough to break inertia ; the card methods, audio visuals, group discussion, horizontal and vertical integration, pomodaro technique, flash cards, blind folds neurobics, minute counting and so many anchoring models of NLP are here to support your sensorimotor well being. Keep your dedication and capacity building attitude and very soon you will do miracle.

19. Afflictions to uplift resources. You can attract your support system. The world is full of great advisers and supporters, you have to leave old haters and blame gamers, and then only you

can create space for better things. No need to increase afflictions in the matter of resource collection, otherwise impatience and frustrations will destroy faith for everything in future.

20. You are ready to reflect self help commands to move ahead with great speed. Just give permission to yourself to respond to every call that excites your spirit of emotional well being. Don't be lazy to think and act according to new thought pattern. Always keep in mind; don't follow the old pattern, make better choices every minute, it's essential to maintain high vibes zone.

EXTRAORDINARY PERCEPTIONS; SENSE THE SUPER SENSE THETA VIBES

See, Hear, Touch, Smell, Taste, engage your all 5 senses to experience 6 th sense related extra ordinary manifestations.

Always remember that you are good enough to proceed forward. Don't wait for perfect inputs and outputs. The secret about universe is simple; you have to move ahead with full faith in your abilities and have to show your best possible efforts. Your efforts are good enough to get anything you want to achieve with the all universal secrets revelations. Your hidden blocks are the main cause of suffering and with the proper repetitions

1. Feel the perfect connection and affection with the present moment. Don't release your frustration and irritation on any matter. The

2. Work ethics and microaction discipline; show your creditability in every micro action and make this habit very clear to you. Habit is what keeps you going growing and glowing.

3. Protect your power sleep patterns; weekly wisdom analysis report

4. Think and talk like a genuine genius; level up and speed up super talks and feelings

5. Be realistic with full commitment; simultaneously learn to unlearn old pain points

6. Promises to keep high zone of joy ride with proficiency and blissful consolidation;

7. To establish declaration and signature events learn the acquisition of emotional memories

8. Amygdala aids in the potentiation of memory traces for emotionally arousing stimuli during their acquisition and consolidation into long term declarative memory

9. Let critics make you stronger ; ignore them with respect and do I3 works; Imagine wisely, Innovate quickly and Implement massively

10.   Don't give hateful response to anyone; hate is the sign of weak mind; no one can put you down to an inferior point to create hate around you.

11.   Affirmation with high five commands;

    11.1 faster manifestations

    11.2 powerful visualization

    11.3 support attraction

    11.4 energy manipulation

    11.5 A3 excellence awake alert active

12.   Genius Quadrant

    12.1 Grow fast and write word bank

    12.2 Glow more and write Tree points

    12.3 Add value with proper vertical integration

    12.4 Raise the standard and maintain zone of high vibes

13.   BOLD signals (blood oxygen levels dependent) and neurotransmitter receptor activities

14.   Natural drive for success and tiny details for micro moments alert

15.   Brilliant priority points and relationship ethics;

16.   Don't make excuse, just execute Best ideas with extra efficiency and better accountability every day do better than previous.

17.   Repeat and redesign ; every time better points

18.   Feel bliss and essence of healing enriched words ; think about precognition, clairvoyance, extra sensory perceptions

19.   You will do extraordinary works if you are committed to great perception making and beautiful response manipulations. Your responses are going to win the heart despite of all stressful situations; now you are ready to go beyond failures and imperfections ;

20.   Take your control over I7 and maintain win win situation in every event

    20.1 Intuition

    20.2 Intention

    20.3 Interest

    20.4 Intellect

    20.5 Images

    20.6 Ideas

    20.7 Implementations

EMOTIONAL AGITATION TO SOUL ENRICHMENT

The soul enrichment is the beautiful culture to adopt. Fulfilment and satisfaction, both the things are not less than bliss. Why some persons are suffering and emotional agitation is also there in the different shades of mood. You can solve problem of emotional agitation and can create a powerful aura to enlighten your soul.

No matter what stay focused and motivated, during times of high pressure. You have to do clear observation of orientation related things, if there are more disturbing things then you have to leave the place or person; always remember you have to lose someone just to create space for new and better. You have to manage time and skills to give peak performance. Just focus on 3 steps rule and achieve soul enrichment.

1. Read the aura and do reiki exercises to clean and charge each and every chakra. The chakra healing steps and affirmations of specific chakra, learn from the Reiki masters. Be a reiki master as soon as possible.
2. Breathing exercises are wonderful to control our mind. The parasympathetic and sympathetic control will become adjustable with proper breathing patterns. Breathing pattern delta trainings with suryanamaskar will change your persona also.
3. Cognitive restructuring skills are necessary for addressing symptom or stimuli related fear, stress, anxiety, depression. Treatment protocol depends on evidence based therapy. Give easy to use solutions and long lasting effect always depends upon affection and assurance provided by other supporters.

The next point to control emotional agitations and to enhance emotional well being, that is 8 point system.

8 points system and Brain reward limbic lobes; Let's learn neuroanatomy and cognitive skills. The 8 points system is very powerful to maintain high EQ level. Actually we are the neuroanatomist and we talk only about the research reviews and patient counselling sessions experiences; there are possibilities of more better outcomes if we get enough time and faith to treat psychosomatic

disorders. Thats why the amygdala, hippocampus and dorsomedial thalamus activity control exercises are very important. Then only the insular cortex sensitivity will subside inner visceral stimulations, gut digestive controls and temperature regulation etc.

Prevent amygdale hijack but don't do past trauma related exposures again and again. Enhance frequent supportive statements exposures.

8 POINTS OF HIGH EQ MAINTENANCE;

1. Set standards and every day think, how you can do better than previous. Quality, quantity and speed everything is important towards betterment approach. Don't allow yourself to put excuses and never set low standards as comfort zone is not a matter of concern in the dictionary of achievers.
2. Accept mistake, improve them quickly and avoid any faults in future vision neurobics. Keep high alert mode always on , as you have to reimagine future success with the current situation. The better version of you is not the matter of future, the best version is here right now. Do the extraordinary work right now.
3. Negligence in delta training will make you weak in creative visualization. The fear guilt grief and lazyness all are the bad factors, thats why delta training teaches you how to overcome fear to reduce all negative effects. Follow the delta training 9 phase meditation commands.
4. Repeat 1000 highlights daily; maintain superimposed sigma diary. Superimposed sigma related commands are very vital, keep them systematically written and in ready to revise mode. Past goodness impact on present command to visualise better achievement in future; that is the theme of superimposed sigma.
5. Move to next level as soon as possible.
6. You are a magnet; you are attracting super success and never say die before final achievement.
7. Glutaminergic pathway control with the help of dopamine and serotonin balance.
8. Be an expert of subliminal perception and alpha introspection. The cognicare neurobics exercises provide opportunities to achieve sure success to socialize and connect with high quality talented and supportive persons.

Now try to focus on to remove the toxic vibes from your life. The potentially lethal words are the main culprits of your failure. Keep yourself away from their affect and bad impact. Prevention is better than cure. Try to understand the essential and constitutional fundaments of social intelligence. Don't get involved into low vibes trap.

We all have a certain degree of intuitive abilities. Intuition is one of the innate abilities to sense things in the world around us. Be sincere to utilizing insights into the science of cogni-skill neurobics. It is very useful for reshaping exercise to restore progressive realisation.

This is how you get to throw away your greed

And honey money trap oriented cheap fighters.

The preventive measures are easy to understand and really very essential, because of increasing ecosystem pollution and thought disorders related psychosomatic diseases. The dirty and unethical environment is the main culprit to ruin virtues and value system.

Have you ever realise that you or your loved ones have spent lots of money on expensive medicines and long listed treatment protocols, over the past few years. That is because of lack of knowledge of preventive measures.

Now be alert, aware and active to understand brain functioning and energy enhancement together.

You can enjoy better life with security and guidance from divine universal support. Just keep your energy and soul powers on high vibes mode, never allow anyone to decrease standards of your value system.

The abundance and prosperity attraction is possible when your preventive measures and peak performance strategies are on implementation mode.

The binaural double induction will create delta effect to subside amygdala hijack. Celestial energy resonates through the sounds of feelings and intentions. Yes better thoughts and feelings can create high vibes and that type of 6th sense sound is best source for healing.

Read, revise, recall, revisit, reimagining, all the statements of modules of this amazing book, again and again. A comprehensive guide book SELF HELP NEUROBICS, which deserves all kinds of praise. This amazing book teaches you how to improve your vibration powers to heal feelings and glorify dealings. With the help of cognitive neurobics the imagination power will become magical to attract manifestations. Imagine being able to achieve enhancement of conscious awareness in mere minutes with almost no effort to deep dive.

Supercharge your confidence with this affirmation guided meditation. The new generation guided meditation with fast command session method of cognicare neurobics, is very powerful to stimulate subconscious mind powers and intuitive powers. The intentions rectification and unconditional love expression capabilities will increase massively. Using this gift to boost confidence, will help you see things from a very different perspective. Universal support, divine security and guidance will take care of your inner soul powers and outer aura and ecosystem by tuning out the negative vibes and cherishing up the supportive positive vibes.

100 POWERFUL AFFIRMATIONS EVERY DAY REPEATS FAST COMMAND SESSION

Affirmations motivate, inspire and encourage us to take action and to realize our goals. The statements and commands that you are going to set, will explore limitless manifestations. Have complete clarity and conviction during reading of affirmations. The magic to manifest fast and achieving abundant thinking is essential for soul enrichment.

1. I am connected to the divine source of the universe.
2. I invite prosperity and transformation.
3. I speak up for myself.
4. I am committed to express my gratitude towards life.
5. I am kind to myself.
6. I allow love to fill me up and guide me in all my action.
7. I am able to let go of the past to forgive myself and others.
8. I love myself and others fearlessly.
9. I am bound to maintain respect in every relation.
10. I am ready to dedicate my life for the betterment of my tribe.
11. I always trust and follow intuition.
12. I trust my guidance by my divine.
13. I see Divine light and beautiful energy in everyone.
14. I am unconditionally loved by my Divine.
15. My spiritual insight is clear.
16. I am open to the abundance and greatness the UNIVERSE OFFERS.
17. I am ready to discover and maintain inner peace.
18. I am ready to let go blame gamers and toxic relations.

19. I am ready to build resilience.
20. I am present and aware.
21. I am productive and creative.
22. I am the owner of my new better destiny.
23. I welcome new opportunities, they help me to grow.
24. I let go of all false belief and false ego.
25. I like to go beyond my limiting belief.
26. I accept myself totally.
27. I forgive myself for mistakes.
28. I am ready to grow and glow.
29. I honour my body as the temple that nourishes my soul.
30. I am divinely guided and inspired.
31. I am infinite and boundless.
32. I appreciate all the ways that I am unique.
33. I accept my awesomeness.
34. I give myself permission to heal instantly with long lasting effects.
35. I have an abundance source of energy to feel amazing every day.
36. I am getting better health signs day by day.
37. I am grateful for the beautiful body and mind.
38. I treat everyone with full compassion to cherish strong relation.
39. My mistakes are proof that I am learning and improving.
40. I deserve the best. The best is here right now in me.
41. I am relaxed and stable and can easily manage my emotions.
42. I am listening more and more to super charged commands.
43. I trust my insight and intuitions.
44. I am ready for intention rectification.
45. I am breathing properly and following 9 phase rule of meditation.
46. I am ready to release and delete all the past pointing pains.
47. I prefer to be at peace with myself and everyone.
48. I deserve to be treated with respect, love and joy vibes.
49. I am confident and successful.
50. I am not pushed by my problems. I am led by my dreams.
51. I am grateful for every well wisher and my heartfelt gratitude towards every one.

52. I am constantly growing and the evolving
53. Wisdom is my strength now and onwards.
54. I believe in progressive realisations
55. Every day I am doing better than previous.
56. I belong to supportive tribe; there are my well wishers that care about me and my worth.
57. I have passion to initiate mission.
58. I have courage to finish all tasks before time.
59. I have self discipline and self esteem.
60. I am determined to take actions on my all best ideas.
61. I am ready to do perfect practice to cultivate values and virtues.
62. I can let this go and move forward to my best goal.
63. I will rise up, reach higher and play bigger.
64. I focus on my best opportunities having the awareness to say no to the unimportant.
65. If I will change, everything will change to serve me best.
66. I have specific goals and measurable tools.
67. I am working on relevant and leaving behind rest silly things.
68. I am very sincere to attend all time bound commitments.
69. I don't want to miss the opportunity to read a book on personal growth.
70. I don't like to spend major time on minor things.
71. I am ready to work for the extraordinary results.
72. I am free from all traumatic events. No post traumatic stress disorder present here in my mind.
73. I am ready to optimize great brain powers with gut healing visceral sensations.
74. I am committed to celebrate god given purpose.
75. I am aware and alert to discover and implement integrative wellness holistic energy approach.
76. I am learning to attain enlightenment and enrichment.
77. I am blessed with numerous virtuous and joyous moments of love.
78. I have a sigma revision plan to maintain discipline for massive quantity of learning.
79. I know the power of purpose is enough to propel me towards the magnificent achievements.
80. Supreme self confidence means willingness to do whatever it takes to achieve and I have this type of self confidence.
81. I am ready to learn extra to become extraordinary expert in my subject.

82. My enthusiasm is perfect to impact excellence in skills.

83. I am giving my best contribution in every relation.

84. I am ready to prepare myself for the big challenges of life as i have advance skills to modify outcomes energetically.

85. I am attracting super powers to cherish golden opportunities.

86. I have reached deep enough to purify my spirits and intentions.

87. I am getting respect by becoming a person of higher values system.

88. I have mastery over manifesting miracles of next level.

89. I am doing multiple revisions of delta notes and am revisiting my better version every day.

90. I am blessed with beautiful money energy.

91. I am impacting so many lives and getting blessings and best wishes.

92. The pivoting and anchoring ecosystem is my best skill to set better changes and choices.

93. I healed and changed and getting validation from right places.

94. I am the product of my better mindset and skill set and now I am ready to launch my biggest projects.

95. Everything and everyone is here to make me prosperous and joyful. Only well wishers are around me to make my spirits high.

96. The urgency and intensity to learn all micro details are here in my mind.

97. I am ready to reflect excellent wisdom as I have enough extraordinary knowledge.

98. My inside vigour and vitality is enough to create victory, the 3 v rule.

99. Stay away from garbage. Never entertain the haters and blame gamers.

100. The enrichment activities for great spiritual character are the powerful tool to lead me on distinction.

WORKSHOP SELF HELP NEUROBICS; HIGH VIBES AUTOMATION MODE EQ

7 HIGH VIBES POINTS

- Cognitive Behavioural Therapy
- Neurolinguistic Reprogramming
- Emotional Intelligence Upgradation
- Energy Healing Enhancement
- Smart Study Techniques
- Women Empowerment Cognicare
- Self Healing Guided Meditation

7 SPECIAL QUESTIONS TO FIND ANSWERS

- What Is The Most Effective Way To Learn Fast And Study Well?
- How To Increase 10x Productivity During Daily Study Routine?
- How To Maintain Accountability And Creditability For Soft Skills Development?
- How To Overcome Fear, Stress And Anxiety?
- How To Excel In Exams With Distinctions And Perform Peak Performance?
- How To Activate Brain Reward System?
- How To Balance Energy Enhancement And Emotional Intelligence Upgradation?

Join the highly interactive workshop

&

Get special benefits.

7 PERKS OF WORKSHOP

1. Special Prizes For Winner Teams
2. Special Cognicare Checklist For Parents
3. Nutricare And Hormonal Balancing Healing Tips For Genius Girls Gang
4. Fast Command Sessions CBT @ NLP
5. Affirmation Mastery Session Modules
6. Energy Healing Guidelines
7. Easy To Use Revision Manual

REGISTRATION FORM

1. NAME

2. AGE

3. EDUCATION

4. JOB @ BUSINESS

5. MOBILE NUMBER

6. GMAIL

7. PURPOSE

Congratulations

Self Help Mastery Guidebook is Ready
&
Implementation mode on